RETOX!

RETOX!

GLOSSIER TEETH, HAIRIER HAIR AND TALLER LEGS

IN JUST 10 DAYS

DR JUDITH FABÜLA

Virgin BOOKS

Published by Virgin Books 2008

2 4 6 8 10 9 7 5 3 1

Copyright © Katie Espiner and Louisa Joyner 2008

Katie Espiner and Louisa Joyner have asserted their right under the Copyright, Designs and Patents Act 1988 to be identified as the authors of this work

Designed by Ghost
Photography by Image Creation

Lyrics to 'Making Your Mind Up' (John Danter/Andy Hill)
reproduced with the kind permission of RAK Publishing

First published in Great Britain in 2008 by
Virgin Books
Random House, 20 Vauxhall Bridge Road,
London SW1V 2SA

www.virginbooks.com
www.rbooks.co.uk

Addresses for companies within The Random House Group Limited can be found at:
www.randomhouse.co.uk/offices.htm

The Random House Group Limited Reg. No. 954009

A CIP catalogue record for this book is available from the British Library

ISBN 9780753515433

The Random House Group Limited supports The Forest Stewardship Council [FSC], the leading international forest certification organisation. All our titles that are printed on Greenpeace approved FSC certified paper carry the FSC logo.
Our paper procurement policy can be found at www.rbooks.co.uk/environment

Printed and bound by Scotprint, Haddington

To myself, without whom none of this would have been possible. I am the sunshine of my life.

CONTENTS

Introduction by Dr Judith Fabüla 10

About Dr Judith Fabüla (BBC3; QPR-nil)..................... 16

The Science of Retox: Science Fiction Verses Science Fact........... 18

SECTION 1: DIET

I've Bought The Quinoa, Now What?...................... 30

24-hour Retox Programme for Zest, Zing, Ping, Fizz and Sparkle ..50

Celebrity Retox Diets: Which One to Choose?...................62

Help! Judith's Secret Saviours.................................. 64

SECTION 2: TOXERCISE

Preparing to Toxercise.. 77

Start Toxercising!.. 86

SECTION 3: LIFESTYLE

Beware of Sleep...98

Dr Judith's Kwik-fix Confidence Tips................... 100

Holistic Retoxing.. 102

Retox Retreat.. 116

FAQs.. 124

Index.. 126

Introduction
by Dr Judith Fabüla

Does modern life often leave you feeling weak, stressed, enfeebled, enraged, lethargic, sluggish, or a heady combination of them all? Does your hair feel startlingly brittle yet frizzy? Is your skin a baffling combination of dry and greasy? Do you manage somehow to have both acne AND wrinkles? These distressing symptoms could indicate that your toxin levels are dangerously low. Research, conducted by myself, proves that realigning your toxins can help solve all of these problems, and more. Certain toxins are clinically proven to enhance feelings of euphoria, self-belief and joy. Sadly, the effects of some toxins are temporary, but with my revolutionary, bespoke, holistic retox plan, you can learn to control them, as they will control you.

Few people realise that retox has its roots in a combination of ancient cultures. It combines Bacchic law with Rasta mores to produce an intoxicating diet scheme that few will be able to resist, and you might just find that it changes your life! There is nothing modern about the art of retoxing. No sooner had the ancient people of the Xxanyxxi tribe learned how to distil and imbibe their god, the xxi berry, than they discovered its mind-altering and mood-enhancing effects – they were quite literally closer to god, and they liked it. Thus the destructive cycle of self-deprivation and starvation came to an end, as these wise people learned that the path to joy and wisdom was not deprivation, but retoxification. We have much to learn from the noble Xxanyxxi. Of course we renamed the xxi berry – what you or I would now refer to as a grape – but man is still enjoying the effects of becoming 'at one' with this humble fruit.

It will come as no surprise to those of us who have suffered from Seasonal Affective Disorder or SAD (I count myself amongst that unlucky number, but thanks to the take-up of my diverse treatment range I'm able to grab an essential day or two in the Bahamas every few weeks) that the seasons play a year-round role in our behaviours and chemical well-how.

From the autumnal equinox to the winter solstice – 21 September to 21 December – a lesser-known condition is also making its presence felt: FAD (Festive Affective Disorder).

This distressing affliction inflicts its consequences on 36.74 per cent of the UK's bi-gendered non-un-working population and just a short-list of some of the most chronic symptoms will raise a brow – eye or otherwise – with many a reader:

- Lethargy – resistance to rising in the morning in particular
- Sporadic thirstiness
- Dry follicles
- Itchy palms
- Difficulty with motor neural patterns (late night fondue- (cheese not chocolate) or yoghurt-making for example)
- Heightened allergic reactions (high sensitivity to Sally Jessy Raphael and Jeremy Kyle, but mild reactions to even Jonathan Ross may register)

If you can answer 'Possibly' to at least two of the symptoms listed above then you're in the high-risk zone as a sufferer of

Risk	No to all Symptoms	Possibly/Yes 1 Symptom	Possibly/Yes 2 Symptoms	Possibly/Yes 3+ Symptoms
Low				
Medium		✓		
High			✓	
Extreme	✓ ✋			✓

✋ Footnote	✋ If you ticked 'No to all symptoms' you are clearly in denial and in need of the retox programme as an absolute priority.

I think we have now established beyond reasonable doubt that the condition is prevalent and needs immediate redress. This no-nonsense, de-jargonised little bible will ensure that you need never suffer from FAD, or any of its many and varied associative disorders, ever again.

Simply follow my four-step programme (strictly it's 2 x 2 steps but four implies a greater progression) to discover a new, shiny, glossy interior you waiting to burst forth from every pore. In just two days you'll realise that you are wittier and more attractive than you ever believed possible; you will also embrace the lumps and bumps that some 'nutritionists' would like you to plane off by seeing them in a whole new light; it will even change your relationships with those you love – sometimes permanently!

A retox can often start with a full-on binge, but not many people are attuned enough to be able to immediately align their *chi*, or their *cheese*, in this way. And that is why I have written this book. It brings you a retox concept that is totally up to date. There is no need for hydraters, peelers, sprouters, juicers, hydroponics or any other type of witchcraft. It is a back-to-basics approach; a completely safe ✋ retox package. Packed with tips and hints, recipes and supplements, meal suggestions and bespoke toxercise plans, I guarantee ✋ that once you have tried retox, you will be quite literally hooked. And remember: retox is for life, but why not start with Christmas?

✋ Footnote

✋ May not be completely safe
✋ We cannot make any guarantees of any kind

About Dr Judith Fabüla

(BBC3; QPR-nil)

Dr Judith Fabüla began practising alternative retox holistic auyveduraurvic therapy over twenty years ago at an infantelastic clinic in Papua New Guinea. He has a PhB in Sunshine Healing, a DDT in Light Channelling and an NVQ in Seeds. He also has all his own hair and teeth.

In this, his latest work on bodily wellness ideals, he brings together centuries'-old writings with inner and outer global wisdoms, which he doesn't so much relay as channel. He has studied for years to attain the highest level of Yo, the ancient system of holistic grading. Dr Judith is Yo-Da.

For further information about Dr Judith, his history and his
collection of trademarked essential wellness and healing
related products, visit his website at:
www.judith-is-fabula.com.

Chapter 1
The Science of Retox:
Science Fiction Versus Science Fact

We all know – we've all been told – that we must detox, but how do we really know that our body is ready for that purge?

How can we be sure that our colon is irritated or our liver frustrated? I've had some pretty angry spots (hormonal, I now realise, not chocolate-related as my mother would have had me believe – another great example of how wisdom about our bodies has progressed), but I've been around for forty-three years and I've yet to have any of my internal organs let me know they're cross. And if your organs won't tell you then who will? What should a confused twenty-first centurion do? Sometimes, sadly, even celebrities can't help and that's when you need a fresh perspective. The retoxified view.

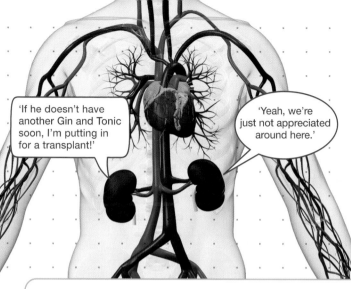

'If he doesn't have another Gin and Tonic soon, I'm putting in for a transplant!'

'Yeah, we're just not appreciated around here.'

What is the retoxified view?

The only way to be absolutely sure you're ready for detox is to undergo some form of retoxification. What my team and I have created here is a ten-day programme. This plan – I hate the 'd' word – will introduce (or reintroduce) you to some key toxification strategies that you can take from the programme and utilise throughout your septo-weekly ✻ routine. The programme is just for ten days. Your retoxified perspective is for life.

 Footnote

✻ Daily to the lay person

How does retox work?

This carefully constructed programme provides a holistic approach to all nine of your toxicable zones: heart, liver, spleen, lungs, kidneys, eyes, spine, feet and hair, so that no imbalance in your hyperbolic chemicalisation will trigger a distortion in your Yo .

This book offers you a revolutionary retox programme. Try it; in just thirty-six hours you'll definitely feel the difference.

 Footnote

 The ancient Bacchic system of balances we use to understand your zonology

Yo

Yo is a mystical system employed by all retox
practitioners. The longer and harder you
practise retox, the higher your Yo level will
become. Alas, it is impossible to try and pay
someone off to reach a higher level if you are
a Yo-Below. It has taken me over twenty
years of tox training to attain the highest level.
I am classified as Yo-Da, and have a quite
fearsome light-sabre to prove it.

However, as I am Yo-Da, I am qualified to pass on just a little of my wisdom to you without being thrown out of the guild. Here is a list of your shortcut to Yo levels – achievable in just one night if you really concentrate.

Yo-Ho-Ho: attainment of awakening

Can you wake up in the morning? Attainment of awakening may utilise any of the following: a loud alarm clock, a partner's sharp elbow to the ribs or a bowl of cold water to the face.

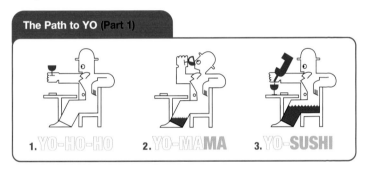

The Path to YO (Part 1)

1. YO-HO-HO   2. YO-MAMA   3. YO-SUSHI

Do you also find that you can often wake yourself up when you have nodded off in long meetings? Again, this attainment of awakening could be achieved by a jerk of your own head as you are nodding off, a scalding cup of coffee in your lap as you spill it, or by your boss shouting your name loudly in your face while banging sharply on your desk.

Congratulations! You have already reached the first rung of the Yo ladder – and so early in the day!

Yo-Mama: letting go of self-consciousness

The next key stage of Yo requires you to lose your self-consciousness or your inhibitions. The key inhibitor that I have come across during my research is sobriety. Facilitators in the One-step Programme towards losing these inhibitions include, but are not limited to: gin, vodka, beer, cider and wine. Simply pour yourself a tall glass of your chosen inhibition-loosener and let it take effect. You are now well on your way to becoming Yo-Mama. But not actually your own mother – unless she is a bit slutty.

Yo-Sushi: letting go of judgemental thinking

If you have attained Yo-Mama correctly, you should have no problem segueing straight up to the next level, Yo-Sushi. This requires you to let go of judgemental thinking. Picture the scene: you are in a public space, usually a public house or perhaps a nightclub. Someone of the opposite sex approaches you. You find them desperately dull, hideously unattractive or with the whiff of the date rapist about them. You cut them dead immediately and move as far away from them as you can.

But, to achieve Yo-Sushi, it is essential that you banish these judgemental thoughts. Perhaps you need to let go of a little more of your self-consciousness? You might still be at the slightly lower Yo-Mama level. Drink one to ten more inhibition-looseners and try again.

Yo-Kel: gaining of special insight beyond words

Now that you are one to eleven inhibition-looseners down, you should find that you are gaining a special insight with people, which is beyond words. It could be simply that words are now beyond you – don't worry, that still counts. You are officially behaving like a Yo-Kel.

Yo-Ghurt: linguistically meaningless conversations

Yo-Kel leads very neatly on to the next level, Yo-Ghurt. At the time, it will seem to you and your unattractive date that you are unravelling the mysteries of the universe, plotting the Middle East road map of peace and deciphering the true meaning behind the lyrics of 'American Pie'. On waking the next morning (or attaining awakening), you will realise that you were in fact simply discussing which member of Girls Aloud is the sexiest. Well done – you are a proper Yo-Ghurt.

Yo-Ga: sitting or walking meditations

By this point you are probably slumped in a corner of your chosen pub or club. You will have a glassy thousand-yard stare you find it impossible to blink out of. Your mind may wander to such enlightened topics as whether to get a kebab on the way home and whether that hot bartender is giving you the come-on. This is a sitting meditation.

Achieving a walking meditation is slightly more complicated, as it requires you to get up, preferably without stumbling, falling over or clutching at the table top as your legs skitter out from under you like Bambi on ice. The likeliest end point of your walking meditation is threefold:

1. toilet

2. bar

3. outside

If you successfully reach any of these, you are officially at the level of Yo-Ga. If you Attain Awakening and find that you are still slumped at the same table, but it is now morning, I am afraid you are back to a Yo-Ho-Ho.

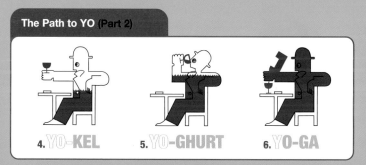

The Path to YO (Part 2)

4. YO-KEL   **5.** YO-GHURT   **6.** YO-GA

Yo-Da: chanting and liturgy
The final, and highest, level of Yo is achieved through chanting and liturgy. There are two possible vocalisations of Yo-Da, and they tend to divide fairly equally between the sexes.

 **Men:** you will find that you are suddenly overcome with the urge to bellow chants more often heard on the coarser terraces of League Two football clubs.

 **Ladies:** you will be strangely drawn to the karaoke machine. Since you have let go of your self-consciousness and your own judgement(al thinking), you will probably choose a song made famous by either Bonnie Tyler or Whitney Houston. And you will really belt it out.

These seven simple steps to enlightenment can be started at any point of the retox programme – and repeated as many times as you need.

Unfortunately, it is highly likely that without proper, intensive training, you will wake up the following morning right back at Yo-Ho-Ho.

YO-DA

7. **YO-DA**

Chapter 2
I've Bought the Quinoa, Now What?

We all know that 'you are what you eat', which makes me a long, cool drink of water, with an above average portion of meat and two veg. One of the most important aspects of my retox programme is the food that you consume.

Before we look at the essential retox foods, I must first share some of my extensive research with you. Harmful foods are everywhere and learning how to deactivate the dangers is an essential preliminary stage of the retox programme.

Oh, quinoa you don't!

Just as figures reveal that 84 per cent of statistics are made up on the spot, research shows that a staggering 69 per cent of the population labour under the misapprehension that quinoa is a grain. Thirty per cent believe it to be the name of the Beckhams' third son. Just 1 per cent can tell you what any holistic nutritionist knows: quinoa is a fruit. Studies conducted by the University of North-East Slough show that if you unknowingly introduce excess fructose into your body, this leads to a build-up of your peptol regulators, which cause split ends.

Quinoa is a bulbous yellow fruit that grows in clusters on small bushes in the Amazon rainforest. It is the staple diet of the endangered pygmy hedgehog. Intensive quinoa harvesting has decimated the population of these tiny hedgehogs, which are no bigger than your thumbnail. Illegal quinoa pickers often throw these defenceless creatures in with the fruit, while laughing mercilessly. You have the power to stop this barbaric practice – vote with your heart and your stomach. Step away from the quinoa and towards Leicester's own Walkers crisps. You'd never see that nice Gary Lineker hurting a hedgehog, would you?

Vegetables: the hidden dangers

Once vegetables are cut, their vitamins begin to leak out all over your kitchen. When leaked vitamins combine with the oxygen in the air they form a de-ionised cloud, which, when inhaled, reacts with the oestrogen or testosterone in your spleen. When combined with oestrogen, it causes the breasts to shrink. When combined with testosterone, it causes the breasts to grow. See table below:

Vitamins and oestrogen–women	Vitamins and testosterone–men
Breasts shrink, leading to dreaded 'fried egg' syndrome	Breasts grow, creating even more dreaded man boobs, or 'moobs'

If you absolutely MUST eat vegetables, swallow them whole. Obviously this is easier with a pea (one portion of your daily allowance) than with a potato – unless you have the jaw unhinging technique of a reticulated python. Believe me, I've met a few who have.

There are certain methods of preparation that will neutralise the ionisation process and contain superfluous and radical vitamin leakage. Wherever possible, deep-fry your vegetables before consumption. This seals in essential toxins. If you must eat sliced vegetables, buy them pre-sliced. The best option on the market today is crisps. Not only have these been sliced in a scientifically controlled environment, thus leaking the dangerous vitamins in the confines of a laboratory; they have also been deep-fried to seal in those toxins.

This scientific double method delivers a completely safe vegetable direct to you, in a handy portable bag.

Sadly, the same principles do not apply to bags of salad.

Since they are sealed, untreated, into the bag, as soon as you open the bag the vitamins are released, and you inhale the dangerous cloud almost immediately. If you absolutely must prepare and eat a salad, ensure that you are wearing a Dr Judith-approved face mask and gloves at all times. The mask and gloves, rigorously tested to my own exacting high standards, and certified with the Dr Judith seal of approval, are available from my online shop:
www.judith-is-fabula.com

Water: nature's poison

Water can be deadly. It is packed with both free and imprisoned radicals, which can wreak havoc on your eyes and kidneys if imbibed in an impure state. Drinking water will flush you out, thinning your blood of enzymes and nutrients, and leaving you weak and at risk from telemarketing scams. There is only one way to safely drink it: frozen.

Freezing water into its constituent crystallised particles, or 'cubes', allows you safely to consume all the water that you need. To ensure that it gives you the zest you require, it should ideally be combined with a clear, distilled or fermented alcoholic beverage. The crystallised molecules in the 'cube' form magnetic particles that combine with the alcohol to turn it into a revivifying tonic. It is then safe to drink as much of this special water as you wish.

Water ready for use ✔

Fruit: just say no!

Attractively packaged, brightly coloured and offered in a range of handy sizes – from single to bunch – these potentially deadly items are usually positioned, blatantly, brazenly, like ripe whores for the plucking, right at the front of your local supermarket. A real blight on otherwise peaceful neighbourhoods, they can often be found loitering outside local shops, on street corners and even hanging from trees.

It all starts off innocently enough: a shiny apple here, a tempting cherry there. It's so cheap, so easy to get hold of and everyone's doing it. Everywhere you turn people are encouraging you to eat more. Addicts can easily manage five a day or even more, in every colour of the rainbow. And it's so casual! Society is going to the dogs (just ask the *Daily Mail*) and the proof is literally there before our very eyes. These people think nothing of casually unpeeling a banana on the

NO!

bus, munching an apple as they talk to their grandparents or even scoffing a tangerine in front of impressionable children.

Luckily, the retox programme helps you to watch out for the danger signs. You used to carry an apple round in your bag for weeks on end – it gradually got more and more bruised until eventually you threw it away. Come on, admit it. We've all done it. People experiment, especially when they're young. It doesn't mean you have a problem. But things start to change, and it's a slippery slope. It usually starts with a few grapes at the supermarket checkout. What harm can it possibly do? But before you know it, you've polished off an entire bunch, mindlessly popping them into your mouth while you're watching *EastEnders*. The next day, you drink a smoothie and it tastes so good – all those zinging berries give you a real buzz. But that kick never lasts, and soon it's not enough.

Your body cannot make or store vitamin C, so it soon begins craving its next deadly fix – the elusive highs, followed by the deathly lows. You find yourself on your knees in a field at midnight, plucking strawberries straight from the bush and cramming them, still covered in soil, into your filthy mouth. You have to leave meetings to eat an entire kiwi fruit (skin and all) that you've hidden in the toilet cistern at work. Your smoothie habit begins to spiral out of control. It used to be that a banana and raspberry could satisfy your craving, but then you find that you need a pomegranate and blueberry to give you the same buzz. Before you know it, the common or garden Granny Smith is just not enough. It has to be pineapples, prickly pears, physalis... dangerously expensive and out of season. One night at a party someone offers you a go on their acai – and the next thing you know, you wake up in a graveyard with a full back tattoo of Mariah Carey, a dry mouth, a thumping headache and that familiar feeling of self-loathing.

Your habit is suddenly costing you £25 a day and it's showing no signs of abating. You lie to your partner about where you've been – claiming you've been at the local brothel when really you have been

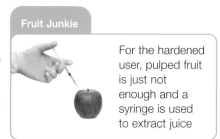

Fruit Junkie

For the hardened user, pulped fruit is just not enough and a syringe is used to extract juice

sniffing bananas in the organic section at Tesco.

But help is at hand. Just repeat this simple mantra to yourself: don't start and you'll never have to stop. Just say no. Because today's innocent apple is tomorrow's tell-tale crimson-stained lips and acid stomach reflux…and that is simply not the retox way.

Banned substances:
Helping you to stay off that wagon

Although I try to be as flexible as possible – in all aspects of my life, but particularly regarding my retox programme – there are some foods that simply must be banished from your cupboard, your fridge and your shopping list if you are ever to achieve total retoxification.

Tempting as these trendy foods may be, if you have any hope of scaling even the basic levels of Yo, you must not have your head turned. Nobody said that retoxing was easy. OK I might have said it, but I was talking about something else.

Substance	'Why is it banned, Dr Judith?'
Millet	It is for budgies, and budgies only
Rape seed oil	The nutritional term for someone who cooks with rape seed oil is a 'rapist'
Quinoa	What is it? And who cares?
Edamame beans	Trying to pronounce it makes you look foolish
Algae, of any colour	Although natural, still against nature. Note: mould does not count as algae, so feel free to continue shopping in the 'reduced' aisle at your local supermarket
Grass, of all kinds, including bamboo	Eating grass is a symptom of nausea in pets
Urine, no matter whose	It's not the 70s
Hemp seeds	Never to be taken in seed form. Complete waste of good hemp. To be smoked only
Nettles and dandelions	See Grass. Note: dandelion is only acceptable when consumed in popular fizzy drink with burdock
Mung beans	For hippies

Warning!
1: seeds and nuts are dangerous and highly explosive
2: the only good berry is a Pillsbury
3: the only bad cake is an oatcake

How to shop!

The golden rule is 'Never Go Shopping on an Empty Stomach'. Luckily, if you are sticking to the retox plan effectively, you will never actually have an empty stomach. But be sure you never take the chance, as it can have devastating consequences. One tragic case study of mine was in such a bewildered, sugar-deprived state, she was in the car park before she realised that she had bought a bag of brown rice with the full intention of eating some.

What should I look for?

You must ensure that all the food groups are represented. If you're not sure what the five key food groups are, they are as follows:

Below is a checklist that provides a handy guideline for the devoted retoxer. I would advise you to steer clear of the fruit and vegetable aisles altogether – it is far too easy to slip up, particularly in the soft-fruit season.

FOOD TYPE	LOOK FOR
1. Mushrooms	Breaded
2. Potatoes	Wedges, waffles, home-fries, curly fries, fried fries, croquettes
3. Onion	Rings – battered and fried, or crisps
4. Cauliflower	Only safe when eaten with cheese
5. Apple	Pie, turnover, cake
6. Orange/Mandarin	Squash, as cheesecake topping
7. Strawberry	Daiquiri, ice-cream, Angel Delight

FOOD TYPE	LOOK FOR
8. Lemons	For gin or vodka based drinks only; aids safe digestion of water (cubes)
9. Pineapple	Tinned in rings or cubes (ideally only eaten with mild cheddar cheese, and off a cocktail stick)
10. Fish	Fingers, battered, breaded, boil in the bag
11. Turkey	Twizzler, mechanically recovered
12. Pork	Scratchings, hot dog, wurst of any kind
13. Scampi	Fries, in a basket
14. Crab	Paste
15. Beef	Corned, tinned
16. Chicken	Nuggets, goujons, strips, Kievs, dippers, in a bucket
17. Milk	Shakes
18. Bread	Garlic, garlic and cheese, cheese

RETOX!

Diet

Skittles: the new superfood?

Reading about the hidden dangers of fruit and vegetables has probably left you feeling very confused. Sadly, we live in a world full of conflicting advice. Every day there seems to be a new rule, and it's so hard to keep up.

It's enough to make my head spin – and I am a practising practitioner with more than twenty years' experience under my Gucci belt. How is the humble retoxer supposed to cope? Luckily, I have been at the cutting edge of research concerning effectiveness testing of a brand new superfood – and can now exclusively reveal my findings.

Eat 5 a day!
Wine is good for you!
You cannot kiss your own sister! Ever!
Eat the rainbow!
Wait!
Take more exercise!
Not as much exercise!
But not like that!
...as much as that!

So move over walnuts, step aside pomegranates and sayonara soya beans. Introducing the new superfood:

Skittles

These colourful little fellas are packed with flavonoids, and contain the exact phyto-beta to non-nutrient bioactivity ratio needed to inflate your cells, reactivate your lipids and conquer your lingering halitosis.

Just a handful of this super-duper food provides you with your recommended five a day, and so much more.

Myself and my research partner (also my mixed doubles badminton partner), Dr Erica P. Kirschenbaumen, author of *Healthy Heart, Dirty Mind*, are on the very brink of cracking the Skittles Code. We have, for the first time ever, successfully stripped each individual Skittle down to its component parts and uncovered the following ground-breaking results:

Colour	Flavour	Effect
Red	Strawberry	Increases virility (especially in men)
Orange	Orange	Improves banter
Yellow	Lemon	Improves hand/eye co-ordination
Green	Lime	Improves muscle tone
Purple	Blackcurrant	Increases self-confidence

Results =

When eaten in a specific, as-yet-undiscovered order, it is my personal scientific belief that Skittles can turn you into a super-human. Making you instantly virile, agile, athletic, strong, supple, confident and magnetically attractive to the opposite sex, Skittles truly are the superest of all the superfoods.

I have gone some way to cracking the elusive code myself, and can now provide for you, exclusively, the first strand of this holiest of grails:

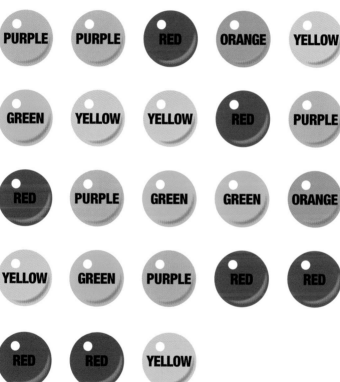

The makers of Skittles are so concerned about the code being cracked and retoxers becoming the first breed of super-duper humans that they have made it scientifically impossible for more than eight purple and seven red to be found in any one packet. This is definitely a clue.

It is worth noting here that low-level retoxers should not attempt to crack the Skittles Code without hands-on help from a registered retox expert. Eating bag after bag of Skittles in the wrong order will simply result in the following

Warning! – Side-effects

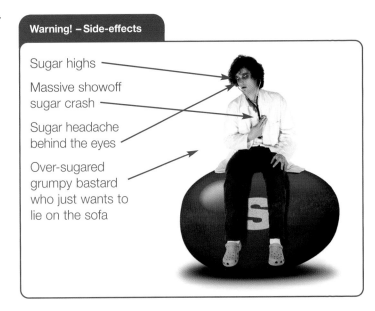

Sugar highs

Massive showoff sugar crash

Sugar headache behind the eyes

Over-sugared grumpy bastard who just wants to lie on the sofa

What does my poo say about me?

What, behind your back, when you've gone out of the room to refresh everyone's drinks? Are you quite mad? Engineers have spent hundreds of years designing the toilet, and we should thank our lucky colours that they have. Once your toxins are properly aligned, your adreonidal gland will begin functioning normally and your desire to shit on a plate and offer it round to friends and houseguests for a closer look should settle back to normal. ✋

✋ Footnote

✋ Note that while I disagree with the term 'normal' on a holistic and healing level, in this case it should be taken to mean 'never, zero, not at all, not in a month of Sundays or a million years.'

Smoothies versus shakes

We all know about the power of smoothies to instantly make everything healthy. Who hasn't succumbed to a shake for breakfast, another for lunch and a proper dinner? But if you're anything like me – and I know so many of you want to be – you've wondered what on earth is the difference?

Simple! If it contains milk (or cream), blend it – you've got your healthy shake! If it doesn't, add a quarter of a banana, a tablespoon of yoghurt and blend it: there's your smoothie!

Here are a few of my favourite instant smoothies and shakes, just to help you get into the right eating habits.

Shakes	vs	Smoothies
Lasagne		Fried breakfast
Nachos with sour cream		Donut – jam
Toad in the hole		Fois gras
Donut – cream		Fish, chips and mushy peas
Steak au poivre		Lamb bhuna
Chicken Kiev		Apple strudel
Lobster thermidor		Beef Wellington
Prawn lakhsa (coconut milk counts!)		Shish kebab

Warning! Smoothies must contain banana and a spoonful of yoghurt.

By law shakes must contain some milk.

Chapter 3
24-hour Retox Programme for Zest, Zing, Ping, Fizz and Sparkle

I try to follow this simple 24-hour retox at least twice a week. It leaves every inch of my body revitalised – or, at the very least, vitalised.

Perceived wisdom tells us that only 10 per cent of our daily calorie allowance should come from alcohol. It is easy to stick to this when following my retox programme. One bottle of wine contains an average of 500 calories. A bottle of sherry contains over 1,000 calories. Do not despair! To keep to this magic 10 per cent, simply up your daily calorific intake from an average of 2,500 calories to between 5,000 and 10,000 calories. The 24-hour retox diet has been designed specifically with this magical balance in mind.

Warning!

Some people who are less nutritionalistically activated than I am find it hard to drive, be pregnant, speak clearly or operate heavy machinery when embarking on the 24-hour retox diet. But just some of the many reported benefits include fullness, intoxication, a surge in self-confidence, an increase in self-perceived attractiveness and a new-found ability both to dance and to talk to the opposite sex.

On waking

Find your most relaxing mug. Fill it with naturally pure filtered water, brought to the boil and left to cool for 1 minute and 38 seconds. Add one thick slice of organic, unwaxed citrus fruit of your choice. For these purposes, the following are all classed as citrus fruits: lemon; orange; lime; grapefruit; lime cordial; orange, lemon and pineapple squash. Allow the water to cool while having fifteen to twenty minutes Neurologically Advanced Positioning (NAP) on the sofa. Pour down the sink.

Breakfast

As we all know, breakfast is the most important meal of the day. It stimulates the liver, cleanses the spleen and mentally fortifies your proto-organisms. Most importantly, it will break your fast (the word itself comes from the Greek break and fast, hence breakfast) – though if you pay close attention to my tips for safe sleeping (see page 98–99), your fast will only have lasted around 45 minutes so far.

The Chinese believe that each hour of the day is traditionally associated with a different creature. Lesser known than the Chinese year, this is the Chinese hour. A full breakdown of every animal for each of the 24 hours is available on my website (www.judith-is-fabula.com). But for breakfast, all you need to know is that the hour between 10 a.m. and 11 a.m. is known as the Hour of the Pig. I accurately predict that this is when you will usually be eating your breakfast. In order to fully

immerse yourself in the energy of this noble creature,
you must internalise it – and as much of it as possible.
I recommend the following pig products for a nourishing
start to your day:

Bacon (6 rashers of smoked or 8 rashers
unsmoked, fried not grilled)

Sausages (6, fried not grilled)

Pork pie (to be eaten whole; 2 without egg inside or 1 with)

Scotch egg (4 normal size or 8 snack size; if eating pork pie with egg
omit Scotch egg as then in danger of confusing your body clock by
introducing the Hour of the Chicken, or 3 p.m., too early)

Pork scratchings (family-size pack of).

Simply arrange all of your breakfast items on a plate (or, better
still, in a bowl) of your choice, and enjoy at your leisure.

Remember, each large mouthful must be chewed at least
twice to experience its full, healthful benefits.

Elevenses

The number eleven held special mystical significance to ancient peoples and must be afforded the respect it is due. Ensure that you stop whatever it is that you are doing at 11 a.m. (unless you are in the latter stages of either Nicotiyama (see page 77–85) or NAP, in which case it would be dangerous for your spleen to interrupt your cycle). Focus on the duality of the number eleven and visualise it as a food item. If you have achieved any of the preliminary or advanced stages of Yo, 11 will present itself on its side, thusly: **OBEY IT**

EAT A TWIX

Brunch

Just as the name implies, brunch needs to be a combination of breakfast and lunch. Therefore, simply replicate your breakfast and lunch menus, combine onto one plate and Hey presto! Brunch is served.

Lunch

A proportionate consumption of vitamins is wise at lunchtime. It will give you that all-important boost, which allows you to coast safely through the afternoon. As I explained earlier, crisps are the safest way to enjoy your vitamins. Advances in modern crisp technology have been so great that scientists have actually been able to recreate full meals and package them in a handy bag. You get the entire experience of a cooked lunch, with none of the time-consuming, fiddly hassle of cooking. Simply open a bag and enjoy. This easy food combining is a brilliant way of getting all your essential nutrients. I recommend the following combinations:

> **Serving Suggestions**
> Roast chicken 'n' stuffing
> Lamb 'n' mint sauce
> Ham 'n' mustard
> Beef 'n' onion

> For those wishing to eat a lighter lunch, the following flavours may be preferred:
>
> Serving Suggestions
> Cheese 'n' onion
> Salt 'n' vinegar
> Prawn cocktail ✋
>
>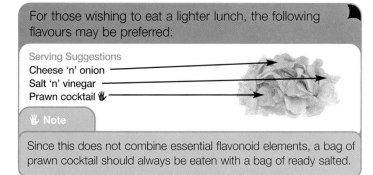
>
> **✋ Note**
>
> Since this does not combine essential flavonoid elements, a bag of prawn cocktail should always be eaten with a bag of ready salted.

Snack

For busy people on the go, sticking to a diet of any kind can be difficult. This is where snacking, or grazing, is essential. If you feel yourself getting weak or sluggish mid-afternoon, simply pop open a Dr Judith – endorsed pro-biontic Baileys Activiate (see page 66), slug it back, and the spring will be put back into your step straight away. You may also find yourself powerfully attracted to someone deeply inappropriate – a boss, a friend's parent or a surly bus driver. This is a normal reaction and simply means that the retox is taking effect. Well done you!

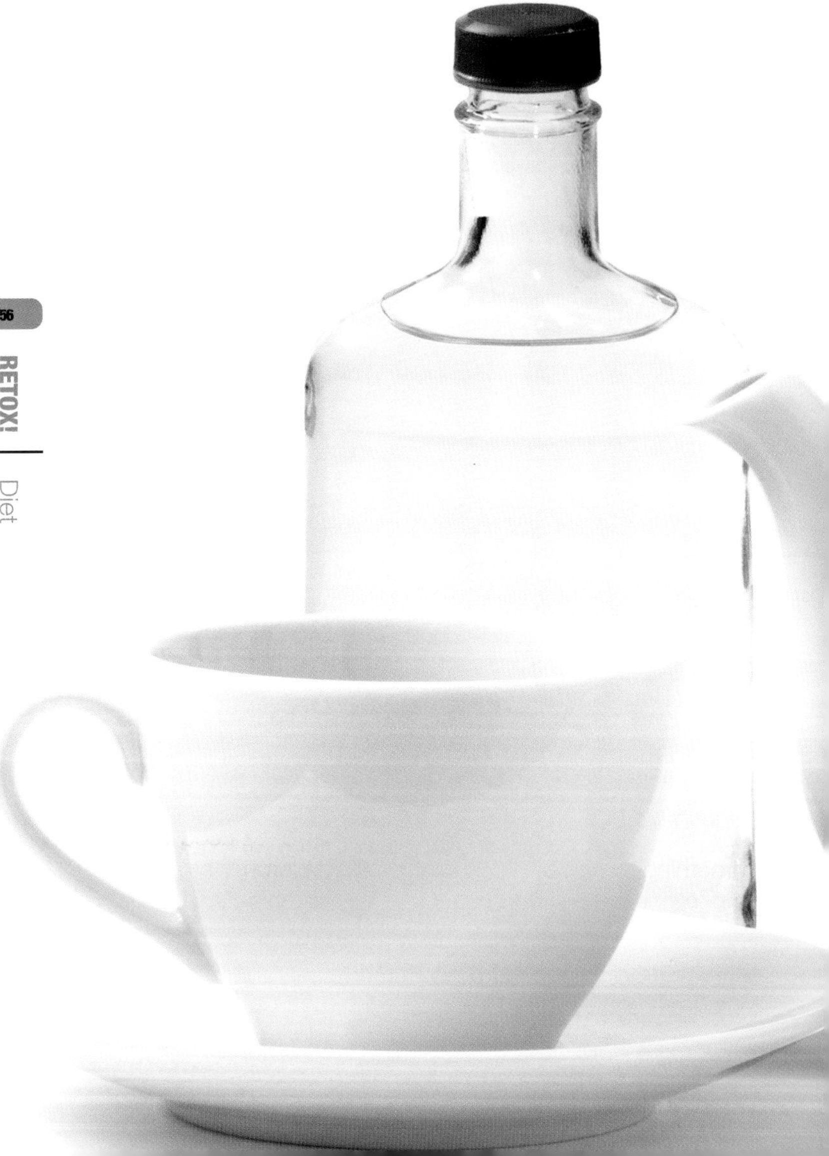

Afternoon tea

Afternoon tea is a traditional, ritualistic process and the retox programme does not recommend that this ritual is disrupted. Disruption of rituals can cause aggressive acne, dizziness and, in extremis, a loosening of morals. What I recommend instead is the substitution of the key elements.

What should be kept:

Serving Suggestions
Teapot
Milk jug
Teacup
Sugar tongs
Sugar bowl

As the liquid tea is usually taken with milk, it is vital that two elements are combined in their place. Fill the teapot with either gin (represents the air element, distilled from berries, for zing) or vodka (represents the earth element, distilled from potatoes, for ping). Fill the milk jug with tonic (avoid slimline where possible – clinical tests have shown that it gives you malaria). Simply pour the 'tea' as normal, adding just a splash of 'milk', to taste. Using the sugar tongs, remove ice cubes from the sugar bowl and add until a drinkable temperature is reached.

Traditional triangular sandwiches should be replaced with something of a similar shape. I favour Toblerone, broken into its component parts and served on a fine china side plate. If this is your first 24-hour retox, do not attempt to swallow the pieces whole. If you are a Yo-ghurt or higher, you should be able to consume the entire Toblerone in one go.

Cocktail hour

If you have planned afternoon tea accurately enough, it should segue (or slide) neatly into cocktail hour. It is essential that you do not disrupt the energy flow of positivity into your bloodstream. Simply transfer your g&t or v&t from your teacup into a large, yet stout, glass tumbler, and continue drinking. The liquid will begin to perform a different effect on your body. When drinking from a vessel made of china or pot, it directly affects your neuronal zones, making you feel relaxed and drowsy. When drinking from a vessel made of glass (more commonly known as a glass), it begins to work on your pro-frontal lobe cortex. Your cheeks will flush, your eyes will sparkle and your volume modulation will begin to falter. As you continue, you will shed any remaining inhibitions, your dignity – and sometimes your clothes.

Dinner

Dinner is an essential meal, second only in importance to breakfast. And lunch. And brunch. Dinner directly targets your kidneys and hair (specifically head and underarm). For balance and equanimity, dinner should be composed of at least one grain, a type of seed or nut, and some replenishing salts. Over the years I have tried multiple combinations, and my recommendation is as follows:

Serving Suggestions

For grain: strong continental lager of your choice

Seed or nut: peanut. (dry roasted or jumbo salted consistently outperform other varieties in both a laboratory and a public house environment)

Replenishing salts: to be mined from jumbo peanuts

My retox team has come up with a scientific formula for ideal consumption in terms of quantity and ratio:

$$\frac{\text{Pints (p) and bottles (b) of lager (l)}}{\text{divided by time in hours spent consuming (TiH)}} = \text{bags of peanuts (BoP) to be eaten}$$

A typical equation will look something like this:

$$\frac{3p + 4b/l}{\text{divided by 2 (TiH)}} = 3.5 \text{ BoP}$$

For those of you not blessed with a degree in mathematics, put simply this equates to roughly three-and-a-half bags of peanuts every hour.

Supper

It has probably felt like a long day by now. But believe me, it hasn't been. A day lasts for 24 hours – no more, no less. Nevertheless, the 24-hour retox is not for the faint-hearted, nor for the lily-livered (nor should it be attempted by anyone with coronary or urinary infections, weak hearts, dickey kidneys, lazy colons, aggressive flatulence or common sense). Come supper time, your body should be fully attuned to the retox experience.

As the sun sets and the moon rises, the stars come out and the alignment of the planets has a direct impact on what you should choose for your supper. If you are on the cusp of a star sign, you must combine the recommended foods from both your signs to ensure your astral wellbeing.

Astraltox Table

Star sign		Ideal supper
Aquarius		Aquavit
Pisces		Cod and chips
Aries		Pint of Young's
Taurus		Doner kebab
Gemini		Double cheeseburger
Cancer		Crab paste sandwich
Leo		Lion bar
Virgo		Large battered sausage
Libra		Big Mac meal
Scorpio		Tequila slammer
Sagittarius		Archers and lemonade
Capricorn		Mystery meat curry and rice

Elevenses II

As with elevenses, only double the significance. Eat two Twixes – or, as this is known to retoxers, a Quox.

Midnight treat

Simply select any of the above meals from the 24-hour retox diet and enjoy again, with one more Baileys Activiate to give you the energy you need to climb the stairs.

Congratulations! You have now achieved the first level of Yo (see page 22) – Yo-Ho-Ho.

Repeat the 24-hour retox programme ten times to complete the full retox 10-day plan

Chapter 4
Celebrity Retox Diets: Which One to Choose?

If the retox diet that I have spent years perfecting doesn't seem quite right for you, remember that you can always tailor-make a programme that is perfectly in sync with your lifestyle. Many celebrities have done just that, with huge degrees of success.✋

Although these celebrities are clearly devotees to the retox cause, at the time of going to print, none of them have answered my phone calls, emails, texts, doorstepping or letters-cut-out-from-newspapers collages and agreed to be the Face of Retox. However, when I have my day in court, I will certainly ask – again. Perhaps she just didn't get my letters.

✋ Footnote

✋ It is probably worth noting that some have been more successful at staying alive than others... so far.

The Celebrity Diet Model	Essentials	Banned Substances
The Supermodel	Booze, fags, coffee, drugs, air	Everything else
The George Best	Booze and sex	Water, mixers
The Karen Carpenter	Air and incest	Sandwiches
The Amy Winehouse	Crisps, salty snacks, ice pops, crack, smack	Fruit, vegetables
The Pete Doherty	As the Amy Winehouse but fewer crisps	Vitamins
The Oliver Reed	Booze only	Yoga
The River Phoenix	Speed ball	Public knowledge
The Princess Diana	Tissues	Other women
The Queen Mother	Dubonnet and gin	The hoi polloi
The Alan Partridge	Bring your own bigger plate	Dignity
The Keith Richards	A little of what you fancy, including parents' ashes	Coconuts (esp. trees)

Chapter 5 Help!
Judith's Secret Saviours

Got a retox emergency? Don't dial 999! Just whip up one of these life-saving recipes. These little gems are my secret weapon, when sticking to the programme is getting too much.

Simplicity is the key to every successful lifetime regime, and mine is no different. At the root of my philosophy are three very simple daily strategies to keep myself on programme:

Morning tonic

Otherwise known as gin and tonic, every day starts for me with a mini g&t. Don't worry about fixing it first thing, an old teasmade can be easily adapted and the proportion of gin and tonic to milk and tea is perfect! Just remember to pop the tonic in the milk slot!

Post-lunch low remover

I couldn't get through those difficult 3 o'clock meetings without my little friend Baileys Activiate. Take a cream liqueur – my own preference is for Baileys, but you'll feel much the same effect with Amarula – and decant it into old yoghurt pots. Pop them in the fridge with a little kitchen foil on top and *Voila*! You've got the perfect pick-me-up any time of day! I always make sure I've got one in my manbag!

Evening glory

We all know the glorious warmth that descends with the sun as it sets. PWE, or Post Work Euphoria, is its very own natural high, but if you're finding it hard to wind down, then just 25ml of poteen can do the trick. The alcohol equivalent of jump leads. We brew our own at home using those pesky tats that always lurk at the back of the cupboard so it's even green! – and I don't just mean the potato skins! In our house the joke is that the parties are always fabülas – but without the poteen I think we'd have to change our surnames!

The Chi's-aligner

It's very common to feel that your *chi's* (or '*cheese*') have been forced out of kilter when you're on the retox programme. Well, you need a chi's-aligner. We're all familiar with the four humours: fire, water, earth and wind. This wonder drink contains all four elements in perfect harmony and it will ensure that you'll be realigned in no time.

Recipe (Serves one)

Earth: 25ml Islay malt whisky **(famed for their peaty quality, this provides the grounding, or base, in this particular cocktail)**

Fire: 25ml Bourbon **(fire water – surely needs no explanation)**

Water: 25ml Irish whiskey **(their reputation for turning gloriously pure mountain streams into wonderful whiskey is irrefutable)**

Air: Speyside whisky **(renowned for their absorption of the moist local climate)**

I prefer to drink each shot separately but if you really need that kick why not pour into one single glass, stir and drain!

The Energiser

Who hasn't woken up feeling sluggish? Catch a glimpse of those tired, bloodshot puffy eyes? Yellow complexion? Red-wine tongue? Well, if you can't persuade your partner to sleep in the spare room, and you haven't invested in my Fabülas Sleep Mask, make yourself this sure-fire fixer. If you can see each other afterwards, I guarantee ♥ you won't care!

Recipe (Serves two)

2 blood oranges
(preferably Spanish)

1 medium-sized carrot
(with frondery still attached)

70ml Snow Queen vodka

Shot glasses **– iced**

Preparation

Cut your orange into quarters,
remove the flesh and discard. Select
your two neatest quarters of peel
and cut zig-zags into one side.
Repeat on second orange.
Take two iced shot glasses from
your freezer.
Remove the carrot from your fridge
or veg rack and wash thoroughly.
Fill your shot glasses with Snow
Queen vodka.

Before going back to your now dozing partner, family member
or housemate, down the first shot, refill the shot glass, and
insert your jagged orange peel behind your upper and lower lips.

Enter your sleeping companion's bedroom, identify the most
vulnerable area of skin available – the neck is ideal – tickle them
with your fronded carrot, cackle through your newly created
orange-peel teeth and down your second Snow Queen shot.

Retire from the room to relax.

 Footnote

🖐 Again, we cannot make guarantees of any kind

Tox treats: more of Dr Judith's Little Helpers

I know that retoxing can be very hard. As with any diet, it is difficult to stick to and it's very easy to slip up. But don't be too hard on yourself – particularly any of you retox virgins out there. It took me literally years to attain the levels of self-restraint, self-purpose, self-discipline and self-satisfaction that I have reached.

I know how it is. Seven days in, your resolve begins to weaken. But do not give up. Sure, it'll be tempting to go home one night, do the vacuuming, eat a salad and drink a glass of water. But no diet is ever easy. You must call on all your reserves of willpower. You will soon find that you are reaching levels of toxicity that you could previously only dream about.

Here are some of Judith's little extras to help you through the darker times. Remember, this is a list of 'freebies' – these can be taken at any time and in any quantity and will not disrupt your retox programme. In many ways, they can only enhance it.

- **Cough medicine**: take a swig whenever your ears stop buzzing and your tongue feels normal-sized in your mouth. The beauty of cough medicine is that nobody will judge you for drinking it straight from the bottle on the bus on your way in to work.

- **Misc. pills**: simply take a handful whenever drowsiness or depression hits. Note that if you are following the 24-hour retox diet, you're likely to hit drowsiness way sooner than depression. The depression tends to kick in two or three days later, around the same time as the self-loathing.

- **Cigarettes**: brand of your choosing, but whichever you decide to favour, try to make them filterless. Smoking is fun, smoking is cool and smoking gets you laid. A lot. ✺

✺ **Footnote**

✺ The diametric opposite of all these claims might be, and indeed is, true.

• **Salty snacks**: replenish those essential salts that can easily be lost through rigorous drinking. A retoxer's best friends include pork scratchings, Bombay mix, Scampi Fries, jumbo salted peanuts, dry roasted peanuts and crunchy rocks of sea salt.

• **Chocolate bars**: I favour the smaller snack size, as you can fit more of them in your mouth at the same time. And, remember, they're called 'fun size' for a reason! Ideal for an any-time energy boost.

• **Cider**: the clearer the liquid, the purer it is (note that this is not true of water, nature's own poison). When selecting your cider, try to steer clear of anything described as 'scrumpy', 'traditional', 'cloudy' or 'to be served over ice'. These types may contain apples. Instead choose a purer, more natural white version, preferably with one of the following in its name: white, wild, lightning, diamond, special. See how the very name has a mystical power all of its own? No wonder that many retoxers find themselves literally falling under its spell.

● **Pork products**: I favour pork pies and Scotch eggs. They are handy, they are portable and they are simply delicious. Packed with the bits of pig that most other products would not dare to touch, just one look at their tantalising egg-glazed (or breadcrumbed) beauty is enough to get you straight back on that retox wagon.

TOXE

RCISE

Chapter 6
Preparing to Toxercise

Nicotiyama

Nicotiyama, or yogic smoking, promotes correct breathing. It is one of the backbones of a successful retoxer's lifetime development and a crucial precursor to the toxercise programme. Rather like the piece of lime in a vodka and tonic, breathing is an oft neglected and yet fundamental element of our very existence. Nicotiyama blends breathing with tar and nicotine to produce the ultimate in relaxed (or completely frozen) lungs. It is also one of the four strands or ureas at the heart of retox.

When looking out on your lungs through the bottom of the glass cylinder – or glass – which now forms your retoxed vision, you will come to understand that Nicotiyama will bring *Niko*, or peace (nicotine), to your brain, it will relax the blood vessels in your lungs (*Ti*) and will help you control the vital energies (*Yama*) that flow like neat créme de menthe through your fully retoxed system.

What is Nicotiyama?

Retox breathing, or Nicotiyama, is the science of breath control. It consists of a series of exercises especially intended to meet the body's needs and keep its chi's in perfect balance. Nicotiyama is derived from the following ancient Lancastrian terms:

Toxercise

- Nico: 'peace' or 'Senior Service'
- Ti: 'relaxation' or 'Berkeley Menthol'
- Yama: 'flow' or 'Lucky Strike'

Taken together we come to understand the full force of Nicotiyama, meaning 'inhalation of smoke' or 'cigarette control'. But this practice of opening up your retoxed inner life force is not merely a question of relaxing deep breaths. It also involves my highly sophisticated, not to say patent pending, 'circular' breathing technique.

I'm going to let you into a little secret. Although this is a very ancient Norse–Western form of relaxation (its roots can actually be traced back to Congleton in Cheshire in the early 1630s), I have woven together a revolutionary Nicotiyama programme by combining this truly dying art with my skill as a didgeridoo player to create my revolutionary breath programme.

But I'm getting ahead of myself. Before we discuss circular smoking let me briefly explain how you get to be a cyclic smoker like me. There are the four stages of Nicotiyama:

1 Peerpressurama: the commencement stage wherein interest is piqued by three individuals eighteen months to two years older than you who, as your first retox gurus (although you didn't know it at the time!), put vast amounts of pressure on you to smoke, thus awakening your love (or vomit) for Regal Filters.

2 Collòeg (Seexth for'um): the stage where the three desires merge to form a chrysalis for the budding soul. The three desires are:

- a perfumed existence (Jazz was the original fragrance for boys, Anais Anais for girls)

- a diamond smile (Diamond White or White Lightning are both acceptable starting points)

- a sparkling, yet tragically unrequited love affair (if you don't count oral sex or any connubial activity near local authority sports grounds)

3 Themorning-afterpill: the stage where the three Collòeg forces conspire to create proper knowledge of Nicotiyama but result in contact with the wrong individual.

4 Nicotti: the journey beyond the merely physical to sheer tobacco joy where Diamond White and gorgeous individuals are left inside grooving to the Nolan Sisters, while you commune with the goddess Nicotiyama in perfect understanding in the car park.

Circular breathing – how do I do it?

That's enough preparation I think, time to get out your mat and start practising. Don't worry if you'd rather not fork out for my especially-formulated ionised Nicotiyama mat, a straightforward mattress will work for now.

Get your kit together, but if you're not sure which way to go, select your tobacco of choice using our astral cigarette chart:

Star Sign	Predominating characteristic	Recommended fag	Chinese sign	Rising fag
Aries	Cool, confident cowboys and girls	Davidoff	Tiger	Marlboro Red
Taurus	Bullish, no-nonsense	Gauloise	Dog	B&H
Gemini	Sensitive but giant mood swings	Mild Seven	Rooster	Embassy Filter
Cancer	Lack of interest in lung cancer and love of mackerel	Honeyrose Blue	Monkey	Honeyrose Vanilla
Leo	Party animal!	Sobranie	Sheep	Dunhill Menthol
Virgo	Hopelessly romantic	Romeo y Julieta	Horse	Silk Cut

Once you've selected your tobacco, gather your preparation tools, which should also include organic matches, and prepare to create your Nicotiyama zone. It's important to remember that this is creating a new you, so let's dispense with the word 'cigarette'. These little sticks of fire are your wands!

Don't forget the ashtray!

Star Sign	Predominating characteristic	Recommended fag	Chinese sign	Rising fag
Libra	Even temperament	Camel Light	Snake	Double Happiness
Scorpio	Dark moods	Death	Boar	More
Sagittarius	Jolly and noisy	Laramie	Dragon	Craven A
Capricorn	Mysterious and secretive	Беломорканал	Rabbit	Cobra
Aquarius	Strong-willed, stubborn	Max	Ox	Gitanes
Pisces	Tend to be romantic loners	Strand	Rat	Karelia Slims Menthol

n the zone

In the zone

Dim the light, stretch out on your mat(ress) choose your first yama wand and let's enter your zone. You might want some light noise (I'm particularly keen on my *Ambient Pavement at 3 a.m. when it's Freezing and you've Forgotten your Coat* CD, but experiment to see what works for you).

Initially you will simply be inhaling deeply, holding for a count of eight and then slowly releasing through your nasal passages. Feel the waves of relaxation wash over you.

When you have bonded with your wand we're going to learn how to breathe in through the nose, whilst breathing out through the mouth, thus recycling the smoke in your lungs and saving you literally hundreds of pounds in the process!

At first you're unlikely to get more than two orbits out of each wand cycle, but as your strength and focus increase you will be able simply to light the wand and have it emitting in your zone whilst you drink, socialise or even sleep!

Once you start allowing yourself this kind of deep relaxation – or, as it's sometimes called, 'addiction' – you'll never want to turn back!

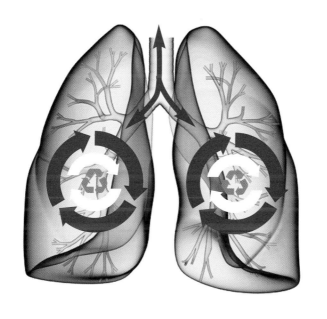

Chapter 7
Start Toxercising!

Over my years as a practising retox counsellor I was constantly being asked if there was a safe exercise plan to complement my internationally successful diet schedule, and five years ago I launched Dr Judith's toxercise! routines. I'm really excited to be able to share them with you here.

We all know the perils of exercise. The risks in attempting literally to lose parts of our bodies are immense. We find the idea of burning witches ludicrous and historically naïve, but what will commentators in the twenty-second century think of the barbarity of us literally setting fire to ourselves when we burn our own calories?

Exercise isn't just dangerous, it's also invidious. Something as simple as forgetting to pick up the remote control before you settle into the sofa can completely derail a retoxing session in full flow.

The secret

My life programme is devoted to helping you through those difficult moments and toxercise is the key to surviving accidental or forced energy expulsion. Starting gently with a basic toxercise session and building up your exposure over a number of weeks you too could be like Maureen Fabula (no relation – no umlaut), professional toxerciser and 2006 champion, who is now able to retox not only whilst she sleeps and swims, but even during intercourse.

What is toxercise?

Simple. It's a dance class with vodka and a splash of tonic. When you can't avoid physical exertion don't exercise: toxercise.

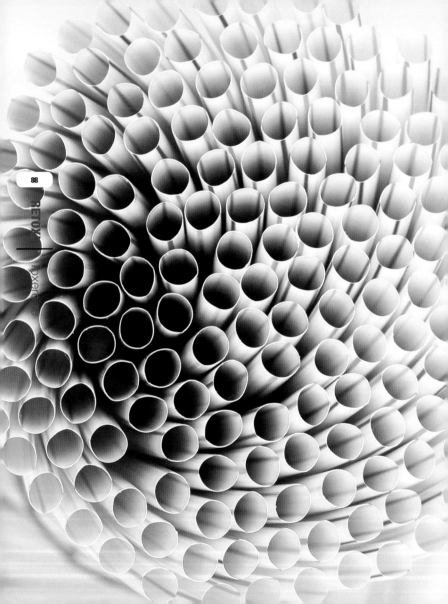

RETOX

exercise

The kit

Before committing to any exercise programme it's absolutely essential to make sure that you're correctly dressed. With the wrong equipment toxercise can be extremely dangerous. You wouldn't dream of going rock climbing without crampons and you shouldn't think about beginning toxercise sessions without the following:

10 x straws: (all straws must contain a single bend; straight straws lead to injuries)

Beginner: all straws must be see-through

Intermediate: begin your collection of different-coloured straws, keeping a large supply of black as a back-up

Advanced: loopy and see-through

Professional: loopy and coloured

Starter hard hat: this is really only necessary for beginners (and available at www.judith-is-fabula.com for just £19.99), so if you're going to be training with friends think about trying to borrow a more advanced toxerciser's initial gear. Alternatively order our toxercise starter kit (£34.99), which has everything you need to get you going and includes customisable rollocks for your beverage of choice!

The basics

Toxercise has three core principles:

1 Consume constantly

2 Keep as cool as a neutralised 🌿 cucumber

3 Co-operate with the music

🌿 Neutralised in this context means deep-fried

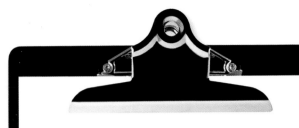

Stage 1 Drinking and dancing! How do I get from the bar to the dance floor, looking smooth and maintaining alcohol contact?

Stage 2 You're smoking! Keeping your feet moving, your lips open and your fingers busy.

Stage 3 Your eyes say no but your body says yes! How to keep dancing and drinking even though you're unconscious.

Stage 4 Where do I put my glass? What to do when the equipment gets technical and how to get drinks to your friends, look great and keep drinking.

The routine

Toxercise is all about feeling the rhythm. From line dancing and R&B to Happy House and even opera our unique ☙ and hugely flexible routine will help you through the most difficult dancing challenges.

We've picked one very special song to demonstrate just how versatile our regime is. If you can make it work with these massive hits the dance floor is literally your oyster. ☙

But if you feel you need more practice go to our website to download other tunes and routines to make sure you're up to speed. ☙

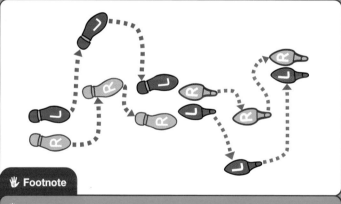

☙ Footnote

☙ No claims can be made for the uniqueness of this dance routine

☙ For technical reasons involving copyright we are quite limited to the examples we're able to take you through but we believe these really are the strongest on the market regardless of those issues

☙ Downloads include: Overture, *Nozze di Figaro*

Case Study 1

OK, let's start with a little warm-up exercise. You're at the bar when the following verse floats across the PA system. As you feel the pulsating beat you pick up your drink.

For this first verse I want you to stand, one hand on hip, the other holding your glass (hold the glass in your writing hand – or use your pants hand if you're ambidextrous), and feel the music. Raise your eyebrows, wink and purse those lips. If you're feeling really geed up you might plump and purse. As you warm up facially you could also tip your hip in time to the music – remember that watering can from ballet classes? It's time to get it out, dust it off and fill it with gin!

Here we go!

Toxercise to it

You gotta speed it up (plump), and then you gotta slow it down (wink)

Coz if you believe that our love can hit the top (dip hip)

You gotta play around (lift hip)

But soon you will find that there comes a time (raise that eyebrow)

For making (plump – optional) your mind up (purse and plump)

Phew! You've got through the first verse! Well done!
Ready for verse two? Great! This time, let's try more movement.

Beginners: nod your head, wink and purse as marked, but this time we're introducing straw contact. Make sure you maintain lip to straw touch at all times but do not attempt drinking. Watch out for the quick left/right on 'about' – it can still catch me out after all these years!

Intermediate: if you're happy with the hip action carry the sway from the waist, flicking the hair slightly at the furthest point of each turn.

Toxercise to it

You gotta turn it on (hip swing and eyebrow rise) and then you gotta put it out (purse)

You gotta be sure (hip swing – optional) that it's something everybody's

Gonna talk ab- (hip swing) out (hip and wink)

Before you decide that the time's arrived (hip swing)

For making your mind up (wink, swing, and purse)

Wow! Feeling the heat? I know I am. Let's add in some sipping, but remember we've still got another verse to go, so don't drain that glass just yet…

If you've lost the raised eyebrow, don't worry, simply try again. Just make sure you haven't spilled anything. If you need to refresh (your drink), go ahead and do so now.

Toxercise to it

Don't let (sip) your indecision (eyebrow), take you from behind (hip swing – double if you're intermediate – and sip)

Trust your inner vision (wink and sip), don't let others change your mind (plump and sip)

You're a natural! Always when we hit the bridge we pick up pace so don't worry if that was the toughest bit so far.

Right: Time for the burn! Real beginners, slip your drink into your rollocks and pop on your hard hat, we're about to head for the dance floor! Don't forget every step you take still maintains total straw/lip contact. Smoking, dancing and drinking is only for the very advanced and not to be tried on this warm-up song.

Intermediates: do swing on all the steps – I know you can do it!

Toxercise to it

And then you really gotta burn (sip) it (wink) up (step and swing)

And make another fly (plump) by (purse) night (sip)

Get a run (step) for (step) your (step) money (step) and take (sip) a chance (flick)

And it'll turn out (purse) right (sip)

And when you can see (step) how it's (wiggle) gotta be (sip)

You're making your (plump) mind (purse) up (wink and sip)

We're really getting somewhere! How did you cope with the new moves I've thrown in? Tricky, huh? Don't worry! Ultimately toxercise loves improvisation – if you want to flick on a plump, why not? Who says you gotta swing when you want to wiggle? The only rule is don't drop the sips; if you do you're not toxercising, you're dancing. And we all know what that means! You've forgotten yourself, lost the programme and you're going to need to take a Baileys shot immediately.

The great thing about Bucks Fizz – and I don't mean the drink – which has too much vitamin C to be safe in a toxercise arena – is the number of verses.

If you want to keep practicing, the rest of the song can be found in my new *Toxercise!* book, available from all good retailers for just £19.99 including my live DVD. This is the perfect practice song with my special cocktail mix running up to 20 minutes on this single track!

LIFES

TYLE

Chapter 8
Beware

Between the hours of midnight and 7 a.m., you will usually consume a dangerously low 0 (zero) calories. Statistics show that five times a year you will eat a spider, which provides approximately twenty calories and a protein boost which will carry you to – and sometimes right through – your alarm. But these are dangerous hours for the retoxer. The toxin levels that you have been so carefully building and maintaining can drop to critically low levels. Luckily, there are a number of ways in which you can keep those toxins pumping, even while you sleep:

# of sleep

- Keep a cigarette smouldering in an ashtray. If you have become an accomplished yogic smoker you will be able to recycle your own smoke throughout the night. If not, a lit cigarette works on your cheese in exactly the same way as incense.

- Keep an emergency stash of mini Mars bars on your bedside table. Under NO circumstances should you attempt to get out of bed without eating one. If you suffer from insomnia, a weak bladder or are in the binge-eating stage of your retox programme, you should be able to make some serious in-roads into a snack-size pack in an evening.

- Leave a glass of wine next to the Mars bars. Retoxers often find that they get thirsty in the night. This has nothing to do with the salty snacks you have been eating, and everything to do with your toxin levels dipping. It is clinically proven that a simple, secret swig of wine in the dead of night is enough to tip the dedicated retoxer back into their safe zone.

Chapter 9
Dr Judith's Kwik-fix Confidence Tips

Although you are young, gorgeous and gifted, there will always be times during the retox when you are lacking in confidence. Usually this just means that you need a little pep-up, perhaps a Baileys shot or a swig of wine. But sometimes – very, very rarely – alcohol just isn't enough. Luckily I am a world-registered confidence tryxter (from the Latin for healer), and have developed the following foolproof methods for boosting your self-esteem and realigning your confidence cheese.

Confidence tip #1:

Choose an outfit that you feel comfortable with and sexy in. Remember that black is extremely slimming. Take time to put on your outfit. Lay it out on the bed. Slip into a hot bath, full of my patented essential oils – potato for calm, nettle for poise, kipper for radiance. Listen to some relaxing music: my *Whale*,

Dolphin and Traffic Noises of the World CD is for sale through my website shop. Take your time to ease your outfit on, repeating my mantra: I am a sexy, sensual woman or man, that any woman or man would be lucky to have. Put on your chosen outfit, and then simply turn out the lights. While black may be slimming, pitch-black is simply unbeatable.

Confidence tip #2:

When out at a party, remember that perspective is your friend. From a distance, the world looks green and blue; it looks like your bus is coming when it's actually the 79, which is always full of those kids listening to tinny music through their mobile phones; and the person in the corner of the room looks smoking-hot, but close-up looks like the bastard child of Alan Carr and John Major. You could be that person! Whenever you go out, simply sit at a different table from your friends or the object of your desire. The extra distance makes you seem instantly slimmer, smaller and more attractive. At parties, always stay in the opposite corner of the room from the person you are attracted to. If possible, stay in a different room at all times. If they keep trying to get too close, simply go home. You will not get a shag, but you will maintain an air of debonair mystery.

Confidence tip #3:

Befriend someone with a glandular problem. You will instantly seem thinner by comparison.

Chapter 10
Holistic Retoxing

If your retox is going to be completely successful you're going to have to channel this programme into all areas of your life. As we've seen with toxercise, retox really comes into its own when the diet is complemented by a holistic understanding of the rest of our lives. I don't know about you, but my home is definitely where my heart is (which sadly means my heart is

splintered, one of the many downsides to being forced to live internationally). I long to get home after a hard day's training, kick off my feathered training mules, and catch up with *Sunset Beach* re-runs, but there's no rest for the wicked (wickedly successful)!

I hope this section will give you some sense of the Fabüla home, but if you want more, check out the shots from outside my electric gates on the Hollywood estate at www.judith-is-fabula.com

Home

Your surroundings need to support you – sometimes literally.
Every area of your house can help you with your retox –
honestly! Take this simple example:

Fridge planning: chuck out that tired carrot and replace it
with a pack of stubbies; they fit perfectly and you won't
forget they're there, only to rediscover them when they're
floppy!

BEER

A Place beer here

B Place beer here

C Place beer here

D Place beer here

E Place beer here

As with the rest of my carefully constructed programme you can decide at what level you want to engage with Re-shui. I'm going to outline some of the absolute basics here. But if you decide you want to realign the whole house I recommend my holistic *Re-shui-ing your Home*: it's a totalitarian look at the house from doormat (always a pillow, for that pre-key snooze after a truly retoxed night) to loft insulation (few people realise that the loft is a space that was specifically designed for the storage of crisp 6-packs).

The simple freshness of seeing the world through retoxed glasses will help you see your home with completely new eyes. And not just that; if you're really retoxing, double vision will make you feel like you've got a spare set!

Retox rezoning

Get started by preparing for the rezoning process. I have designed rezoning lenses (r.r.p. £25.00 at the website), but if you're keen to start you could ask to borrow a friend's glasses. If you do choose this route please make sure they're sufficiently short-sighted for you to get a headache after a few moments looking through the specs. Pop the glasses into your hand/manbag along with two sets of keys (making sure that only one set will get you back inside the front door). Add a couple of scarves, a highlighter pen and a pair of mittens. We're ready to Re-shui!

Re-shui essentials:
Keys x 2 sets
Scarves x 2
Highlighter pen x 1 (preferably neon yellow)
Lenses/glasses x 1
Mittens, 1 pair

Now grab your bag and exit the front door. Walk to the pavement at least two doors away from your front door and execute the following preparatory stages:

1 Tie your legs together just above the knees

2 Pop one of the mittens onto the hand you do not write with

3 Using your free hand tie your non-free, mittened hand in a sling, remembering to keep your handbag on your shoulder so that the arm slightly restricts access to the receptacle

4 Place the glasses on your nose

5 Put the second mitten on your free hand

You are now ready to begin:

Phase One
Approach the front door as quickly as you can, trying simultaneously to remove your keys from your bag. Can you easily identify which door is yours?

Are you hampered in your approach? Be especially vigilant for bush scratches, fence gouging to the thighs and mistaking your neighbour's front door for your own.

Lesson One
Always make sure your front door is completely identifiable; think about an unusual colour, perhaps a stripe? List all the

potentially aggressive objects in the approach. If they can be moved do so, but don't be afraid to chop down your assailant, even if it's a berberis or a rose bush.

Phase Two
On arrival at the correct door it is highly unlikely you have been able to get hold of your keys because of the mittens and the sight restriction. How able are you to identify the right set by feel? This is where the second set truly comes into its own. If you haven't attached a small furry animal or Thorpe Park key ring you won't be able to tell if you have the correct keys until you are trying them in the lock, wasting valuable seconds lingering on the doorstep.

Lesson Two
Pick a key ring that feels different. Don't be fooled into thinking that colour will help. When you're peering into your bag or feeling in your pockets that lovely shade of fuchsia simply won't help you. My personal favourite is the Nana Mouskouri glasses ring, but you might prefer something from my Neil Sedaka or Nolan Sisters collection. Remember, when you're selecting you must keep your eyes shut! It's all about the feel…

Phase Three
You're inside! Congratulations! But you can't relax. You have two more stages before bed:

A Finding a snack in the kitchen
B Locating your bed, or a suitable sleeping surface

This is what you have to do:

A Make your way confidently through your hallway or lounge towards the kitchen door. Keep a mental note of the surfaces you ricochet off on your way to the door. When you arrive bruised and battered in the kitchen make your way to the fridge. Is there a Re-shui pack (see opposite page) on the top shelf? (It should be clearly marked with a mini Babybel.) If not, you have failed phase 3A.

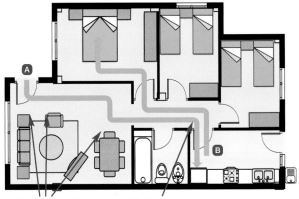

Warning: **Sharp edges to avoid**   Warning: **Sharp turns**

NB: We recommend you place refelctive strips onto your carpet as shown above

B Leave the kitchen and make your way to the nearest soft surface. Is the route to the bedroom clearly marked? (Following aeroplane evacuation principles, emergency reflective strips should be guiding you to your bed.) If not lie down immediately on the sofa and attempt no more movement. You have failed phase 3B.

Lesson Three

Preparation is everything. Whether you're indicating the emergency sleep exits with neon strips and arrows  or a simple first aid kit, a skilled practitioner is a retoxer with a plan.

The first aid, or Re-shui pack, is a vital part of every retoxing household. It should contain:

Re-shui first aid pack:

2 coins (chocolate)

1 cheese and Berocca sandwich (Marmite optional)

1 ready-mixed gin and Resolve in a cup with straw

1 pack Monster Munch (pickled onion flavour)

It must be kept in a sealed container, in the fridge with a 'beacon' mini Babybel on top.

 Footnote

 Once again, check out the emergency routing kit on my website, a securitynecessity and just £18.99

Important note: exposure to the chemicals in household cleaners radically alters your toxin levels. The safest thing you can possibly do is to stay away from them at all costs.

Help! I keep forgetting my morning routine!
How to organise a retoxed bathroom

The dedicated retoxer knows that spending anything more than five minutes in the bathroom is frankly a waste of time. You could be using those precious additional minutes for more NAP time (see page 52). My retox bathroom tips may save you time, but they in no way cut any corners when it comes to personal hygiene or grooming. Don't believe me? Read on!

Bathing and showering

As I have already explained, water is extremely dangerous and only safe to be consumed in cube form. However, it is equally dangerous for you to try and immerse yourself in it. Clinical trials at my secret laboratory in the Seychelles have shown that prolonged exposure to water wreaks havoc with your lymphatic drainage. Tiny particles of water easily pass through your skin pores, causing you to swell from the inside. If you've noticed that you're carrying a little extra weight recently (possibly since embarking on my retox programme), it is almost certainly a direct result of excessive exposure to water. Women tend to swell around the hips and thighs, while men are more likely to retain excess bath water around the stomach.

Dr Judith's retox alternative:

Deodorant: or 'shower in a can' as it is also known. Simply strip down to your underwear and apply liberally: 3/4 of a can applied across, over and round the body should be sufficient. Do not neglect your feet! Pay particular attention to pulse points (ears, wrists, neck, palms, kneepits) and adolescent problem areas such as underarms and crotch. If you are in the later stages of retox, follow these same simple steps, but do not remove your clothes first.

Personal hygiene
See opposite.

Ladies, if you're still not feeling so fresh after your rejuvenating shower in a can, spritz the air with a cloud of Toilet Duck or Cillit Bang and walk through the fine mist, allowing it to settle on clothes and hair. Choose Pine Fresh for stylish confidence, or Summer Meadow for flirty, youthful exuberance. Remember to keep your eyes and mouth tightly closed for this spritz. Your eyes are almost certainly red enough as it is.

Grooming

LADIES
1 Using the tip of your forefinger, wipe briskly under both eyes, removing any traces of yesterday's mascara. Reapply today's mascara.

2 To freshen breath, smoke a menthol cigarette.

3 Leave bathroom.

GENTS
1 Hastily fork fingers through hair. If hair is particularly unruly, lick or spit on fingers and/or palms first.

2 Check self in mirror. Make guns out of aforementioned fingers and fire twice at self in mirror. Wink once.

3 Leave bathroom.

RETOX! | Lifestyle

Facials

Although we wish it weren't true I'm afraid beauty is sometimes only skin deep, but with my facial regime and my patented products ✋ you can always present your best side to the world. You won't believe how good you'll look in just fifteen minutes!

Cleansing pack:
1 x avocado
1 x organic egg (preferably duck)
2 vials of good-quality vodka
6 x plump vine tomatoes (blended)
1 tsp Tabasco
pinch sea salt
pinch black pepper
1 x stick of celery (optional)

Cleanse:
Take a pan and boil the egg for $4^1/_2$ minutes. Whilst this is boiling combine the vodka, blended tomatoes, sea salt, pepper and Tabasco in a glass. If you have chosen to keep the celery, place the celery in the glass.

When the egg is cooked drink the fruit cocktail ✋ (remember tomato is a fruit) and consume the egg. This will give you a gorgeous morning glow; it will scrub out your stomach – and the egg? It's for your hair! Never slept under a duck-down duvet?

Tone:
Few people are familiar with the etymology of 'tone': it's actually a bastardisation of 'tonus', which is the Latin for espresso. This second, invigorating stage of my morning cosmetic programme is a quick caffeine shot. Your eyes will sparkle and your pores will open. You're ready for moisturisation.

✋ Footnote

✋ Patent not pending   ✋ Discard the celery, it is purely decorative

Moisturise:

The world's finest moisturisers are all constructed from one bean: the cocoa bean. Its soothing and enriching qualities are unsurpassed. The common misconception is that this process takes place externally, but for the qualities of the bean to be truly felt they must be ingested. Moisturisation does require a high bean content treatment, therefore. My favourite is Green & Black's Maya gold (100g), but if you're in a fix you can make do with Bournville.

This leaves you ten minutes for the crucial part of any retox facial-cleansing routine. You will need (regardless of sex):

- Touche Éclat
- Mac Studio Fix
- Vaseline (preferably menthol)

1 Dot the concealer under the eyes, around the nose and over any pimply points.

2 Dab face and neck with Studio Fix and blend. Apply Vaseline to the lips and teeth – it'll give you that gorgeous slip-free smile and if you've gone for the menthol as recommended you'll no longer need to clean your teeth!

If you're a boy this will suffice but don't feel you can't follow through the programme if you want to; I'm no one without my guy-liner!

1 Apply smudge of eye-shadow with brush

2 Apply eye-liner

3 Apply mascara, staring into your own breasts in the mirror to avoid splodges (guys, borrow a friend or partner's breasts – a pair you're familiar with will probably work best)

4 Lip gloss, a girl's best friend, and if you get a good flavour as recommended you're keeping up your retox intake as you make up.

My goodness, I wouldn't have recognised you! Go out there and knock them dead. And when you get home tonight don't worry about make-up removal. Your pillow will do that for you!

Chapter 11
Retox Retreat

It is so true that any diet can be difficult sometimes. Self-discipline, motivation, self-deprivation; the changing from one lifestyle to another; trying to work the new regime round your normal daily routine. Desperately trying to stay off that wagon and keep away from fruit.

Sometimes what you need is a little bit of a boost, to get away from it all, recharge your batteries and have a nice long swim in Lake Me. My Retox Retreat offers a Total Retox Experience on the utterly fabulous Fabulous Island. Fabulous Island is a little slice of paradise situated just off the coast of Belize, and as such is exempt from British tax laws – and indeed any other laws.

We offer a holistic programme of retox, including my patented 24-hour diet for the full 7 days (and twice on Tuesdays and Saturdays) and toxercise. Me and my team of dedicated retoxperts create a unique programme to suit your personal needs and address which specific part of you needs retoxing – mind, body, spirit or all of the above. Over the course of one sun-drenched, honey-glazed week, we will unblock your okras, massage your auras and titillate your orbs. Extensive and exceptional dezoning is guaranteed. While many other retreats like to focus on fasting, with retox, the emphasis is on slowing.

Here is an outline of what you can expect during your week's stay on Fabulous Island.

Inspirational talks

Every evening I give a special motivational talk, sharing with the select group my research, my new findings and my latest holiday snaps. For a small additional fee, I also conduct special one-to-one sessions in my yurt or in the Jacuzzi. Please note that these sessions are often heavily over-subscribed and clients are selected at my own discretion. Send a recent photograph of yourself in a bikini, along with vital statistics and marital status, and I will contact you personally to let you know whether your application has been successful. Please note that by a peculiar, as yet unexplained scientific coincidence, male applicants have been approximately 100 per cent less successful than females in securing a personal audience with me.

Colonic therapy: not going to happen

For my feelings on messing about with people's colons, please see the 'What does my poo say about me?' section on page 47. Poking about in excrement? Two words for you people: sick and wrong. Wait, does that count as three words?

Weight loss

Retoxers who stick to the liquid diet regime option report an almost universal temporary weight loss. Retoxers who stick to any of the dietary programmes at all report a universal lack of caring about whether they have lost weight or not.

Massage

My revolutionary massage technique is clinically proven 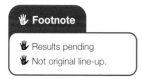 to reduce cholesterol, lower blood pressure, regulate breathing and calm mood swings. A similar effect has been noted on patients when stroking a puppy or a kitten. Therefore I call this my 'Stroking the Puppies' technique. Because of the direct connection between the thorax and the pre-perotinoidal glands, which control blood flow and heart-rate, I always focus primarily on the mammary area for my deep-tissue massage. It is important to note that this technique has not yet been clinically trialled on men, so I am only able to perform this particular therapy on ladies. Tests have shown it to be particularly efficacious on women with a C cup or higher.

Toxercise sessions

To help you toxercise to the very best of your ability, Bucks Fizz will perform their 1981 Eurovision-winning smash hit 'Making Your Mind Up' at 1 p.m., 3 p.m., 5 p.m., 6 p.m., 7 p.m., 10 p.m., 10.15 p.m., 11 p.m., 11.30 p.m. and midnight daily. We will take you through the toxercise routines and provide all the kit and drinks necessary for the full work-out.

Footnote

- Results pending
- Not original line-up.

RETOX!

Lifestyle

Just chill out

Fabulous Island enjoys 300 days of sunshine per year, and crystal-clear waters lap the edges of palm-fringed beaches. Each individual retoxed bunker is equipped with thick blackout curtains so that the bright sunshine does not hurt

your eyes. A high perimeter fence runs the entire length of the resort to ensure that you cannot enter the water (nature's poison), even if you do have a few too many Baileys Activiates with your elevenses. Each bunker is kitted out with a 42-inch plasma-screen television, cable TV, full box sets of all the Police Academy movies and emergency retox snack boxes (fully equipped with salty snacks, Mars bars, pork pies and gin) to ensure that you never need to leave your double-double-king-size bed.

How to book

For full details of my Wellness Retox Retreats, log on to my website, www.judith-is-fabula.com. A one-week, all-inclusive retreat costs from as little as £5,000.

The Retox Retreat runs for ten months of the year. Please note that I am only contractually obliged to appear by satellite link-up.

☙ Footnote

☙ Does not include flights, connections, food, drink or accommodation. Supplements apply

Don't forget to visit my web-site!

You've been done

FAQs

Q: I keep getting back on the wagon. How do I get off?

A: This is a question I get asked all the time – and there's only one answer that's guaranteed to work. Check in for my 'Retox Revival' course. After thirty-six hours in my office you'll wonder how you ever survived without alcohol.

Q: I love the diet but I've started to resemble Pat Butcher. What do you suggest?

A: Ditch the earrings and you'll instantly lose ten pounds! Also remember that the camera adds ten pounds, so throw away your video camera, digital camera, mobile phone and webcam. Voila! An instantly slimmer, more confident you. Better still, you're free to start the programme all over again.

Q: Help! I have my wedding coming up – can you help?

A: Naturally. Dr Judith's Hen Packet is available for just £300 (per head, photographs of bride and bridesmaids must be supplied in advance).

Q: My husband is in an alcohol induced coma after attempting your 24-hour plan. Do you have the name of a good lawyer?

A: Yes.

Q: I have come back from the Retox retreat pregnant, and you were the only man on the island (which your website did not make clear). You are not answering my letters or emails and you seem to have changed your mobile phone number. This is not funny Judith. Or should I say Jeremy. Supply an address where the CSA can contact you before my due date of December 17th?

A: You will not be surprised to hear that this is the most FA of my FAQs. I am constantly pursued by fans, groupies, well-wishers, ill-wishers, gold diggers, crackpots, whackjobs and charlatans. You must supply name, age, vital statistics and recent head and full length body shot before I can move forward with your frankly outrageous claim. I know it breaks the hearts of ladies all over the world, but I must reiterate that I am a happily married man.

Q: I think I have cracked the Skittles Code but I've invested £250,000 of my wife's inheritance in the process and my legs no longer support my weight. What should I do?

A: Easy! Lose weight and get rich kwik with my easy to follow guide:

> Step 1) Let's work together to make your wife famous. Simply send me her photo and I'll send you an application form for my new prime-time TV series *Fabülas Lives*.
>
> Step 2) Take out one of my interest free ♨ Fabülas Loans
>
> Step 3) Jump off a cliff. Your wife will get your life insurance and you'll never think about your weight again! And don't worry – I'll make sure the little lady is taken care of.

♨ Footnote

♨ Free for the first 2 weeks
and then APR 178% PA

INDEX

A
B
C
D
E
F

Fabüla, Judith 1–128
    Bin, Dusty (mother)
    Bros: see Moss
    Brunos I have loved: Brooks;
        Frank; Tonioli; Vincent
    Criminal record see Eurovision
    Drugs scandal(s): codeine;
        copydex; crystal meth; heroin
        (hillbilly); Night Nurse
    Early years see School, Drugs
        scandals
    Eurovision 1978, Belgian entry for
    Ex-
        -Change (French) see Early
               years
        -Communicated
        -Hibitionism see pages 1–128
             inclusive
        -Istential angst
        -Girlfriends
        -Local Authority
        -Onerated from all wrong doing
             (see Exxon Valdez)
        -Pletives used against me in
             courts of law
        -Treme ('More than Words',
             how to play on an
             acoustic guitar)
        -Traordinary rendition, my
             sanctioning of in
             Retox programme
        -Wives
        -Xon Valdez (my role in)
    Germaine: Germolene; Greer;
        Jackson; Stewart
Musical Influences: Chas and Dave
    ('Snooker Loopy'), Hammer, MC
    ('U Can't Touch This'), Marx, Richard;
    Medeiros, Glen; Oldfield, Mike ('Moonlight
    Shadow')
Moss Bros
Parents: see Bin, Dusty and Rogers, Ted
Rehab: 1992, 1993, 1994–5, 2007
Religion: The Way of: Howard (see
    Howard's Way); Tao
Rogers, Ted (father)
School: days; girls; uniforms available
    online
Spiritual influences: Aloud, Girls; Charlie
    (Red); Fries, Scampi; Jazz; Lady Queen Di
    Princess of our Hearts; Ladysmith Black
    Mambazo; Lynx (Africa); Musk, White
World tour: 1983, 1984, 1985, 1997,
    1999, 2001–9 (ongoing)